GET ACTIVE!

BUILDING SKILL

I0895111

Written by Valerie Harvey

KidHaven PUBLISHING

Published in 2027 by
KidHaven Publishing, an Imprint of Greenhaven Publishing, LLC
2544 Clinton St., Buffalo, NY 14224

© 2026 BookLife Publishing Ltd.

Written by: Valerie Harvey
Edited by: Elise Carraway
Designed by: Amy Li

All facts, statistics, web addresses, and URLs in this book were verified as valid and accurate at time of writing. No responsibility for any changes to external websites or references can be accepted by either the author or publisher.

Cataloging-in-Publication Data

Names: Harvey, Valerie.
Title: Building skill / Valerie Harvey.
Description: Buffalo, NY : KidHaven Publishing, 2027. | Series: Get active! | Includes glossary and index.
Identifiers: ISBN 9781534570856 (pbk.) | ISBN 9781534570863 (library bound) | ISBN 9781534570870 (ebook)
Subjects: LCSH: Athletic ability--Juvenile literature. | Physical fitness--Juvenile literature. | Sports--Psychological aspects--Juvenile literature.
Classification: LCC GV436.H378 2027 | DDC 613.71--dc23

All rights reserved.
No part of this book may be reproduced in any form without permission in writing from the publisher, except by a reviewer.

Printed in China

CPSIA compliance information: Batch #QS27KH: For further information contact Greenhaven Publishing LLC at 1-844-317-7404.

Please visit our website, www.greenhavenpublishing.com.
For a free color catalog of all our high-quality books,
call toll free 1-844-317-7404
or fax 1-844-317-7405.

Find us on

Image Credits. All images are courtesy of Shutterstock.com, unless otherwise stated.

Recurring – Tatiana Kubara, VVadi4ka. Cover – Sergey Ryzhov. 2–3 – jstudio. 4–5 – BearFotos, Daisy Daisy. 6–7 – PeopleImages, Sergey Novikov. 8–9 – kornnphoto, polkadot_photo. 10–11 – BearFotos, SeventyFour. 12–13 – jstudio, New Africa. 14–15 – FamVeld, Lucky Business. 16–17 – 24K-Production, PatrickLauzon photographe. 18–19 – Brocreative, VicVic Liu. 20–21 – Drazen Zigic, ZR10. 22–23 – New Africa, stockpexel.

CONTENTS

Words that look like <u>this</u> can be found in the glossary on page 24.

TIME TO GET ACTIVE!

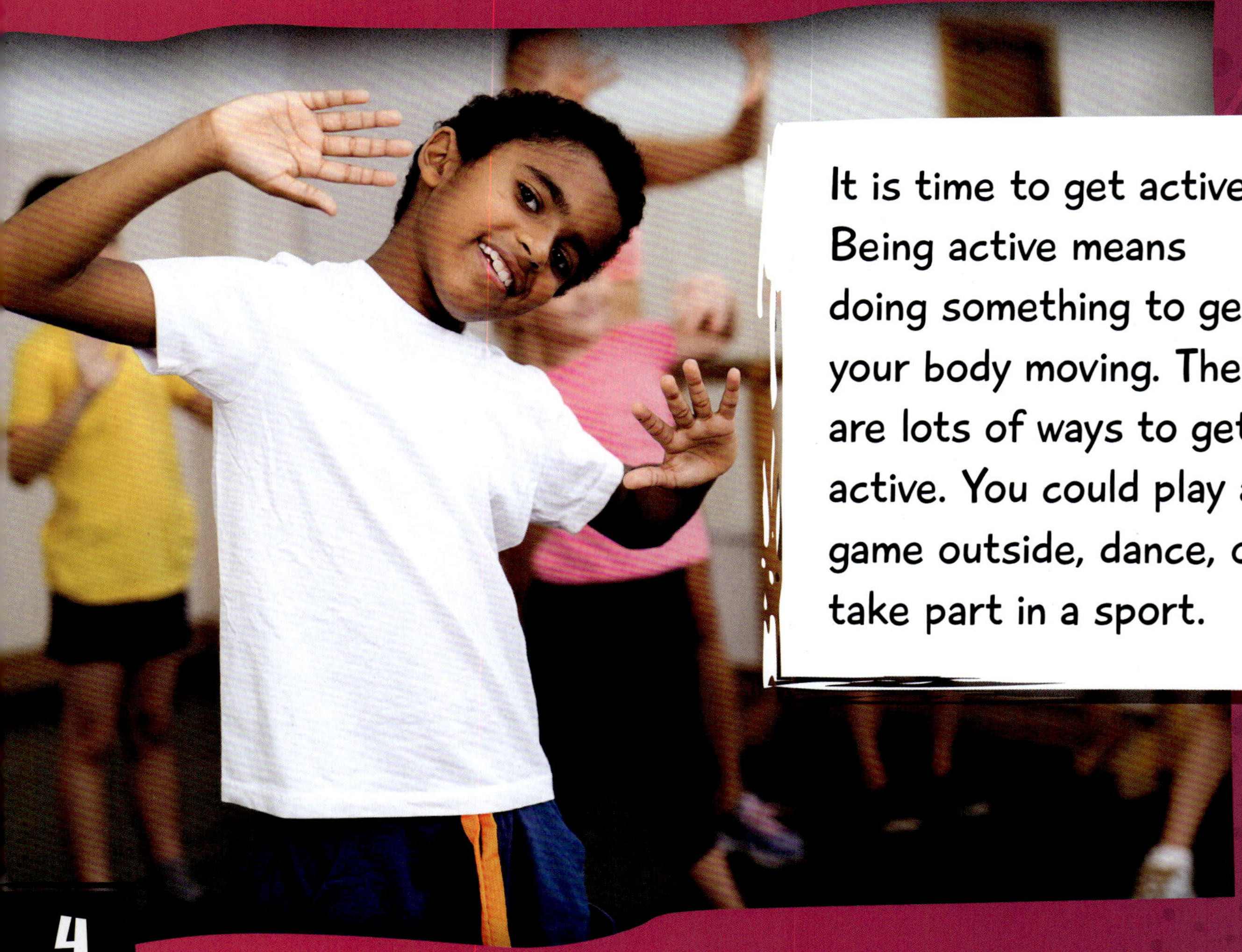

It is time to get active! Being active means doing something to get your body moving. There are lots of ways to get active. You could play a game outside, dance, or take part in a sport.

Getting active is a good way to build all kinds of skills. Some skills use your body. Other skills use your brain. Let's build your skills and have fun doing it!

WHAT IS SKILL?

A skill is something you learn to do really well. You probably already have all kinds of skills. You get skills by practicing. The more you work on your skills, the better they become!

In sports, skills help you play better and have more fun. Sports skills can include throwing, catching, or even communicating with your team. Everyone can improve their skills with practice.

BALANCE

Balance means staying steady and not falling over. In sports, balance helps you run, jump, and change direction. Balance is important for kicking a ball, riding a skateboard, and doing gymnastics.

Someone who wants to have good balance needs strength in their muscles. Strong muscles help you to control your movements. You can practice your balance by standing on one foot.

Parts of your inner ears are involved with helping you balance.

FLEXIBILITY

Flexibility is how easily your body can bend and move without getting hurt. Being flexible helps you dance. It helps you reach for a ball. It makes it easier to twist, turn, and stretch during games too.

When you are flexible, your muscles and joints feel good and work easily. You can improve flexibility by doing gentle stretches, such as touching your toes or reaching for the sky.

Light stretching before exercise helps to warm your muscles up.

COORDINATION

Coordination means your body parts work together smoothly to do something. Coordination helps with movements such as swinging a tennis racket, throwing a baseball, or hitting a golf ball.

Coordination uses the link between your brain and your muscles. Good coordination helps your body do tricky movements without mistakes. You can practice your coordination by throwing and catching.

The part of your brain that controls coordination is called the cerebellum.

CALCULATION

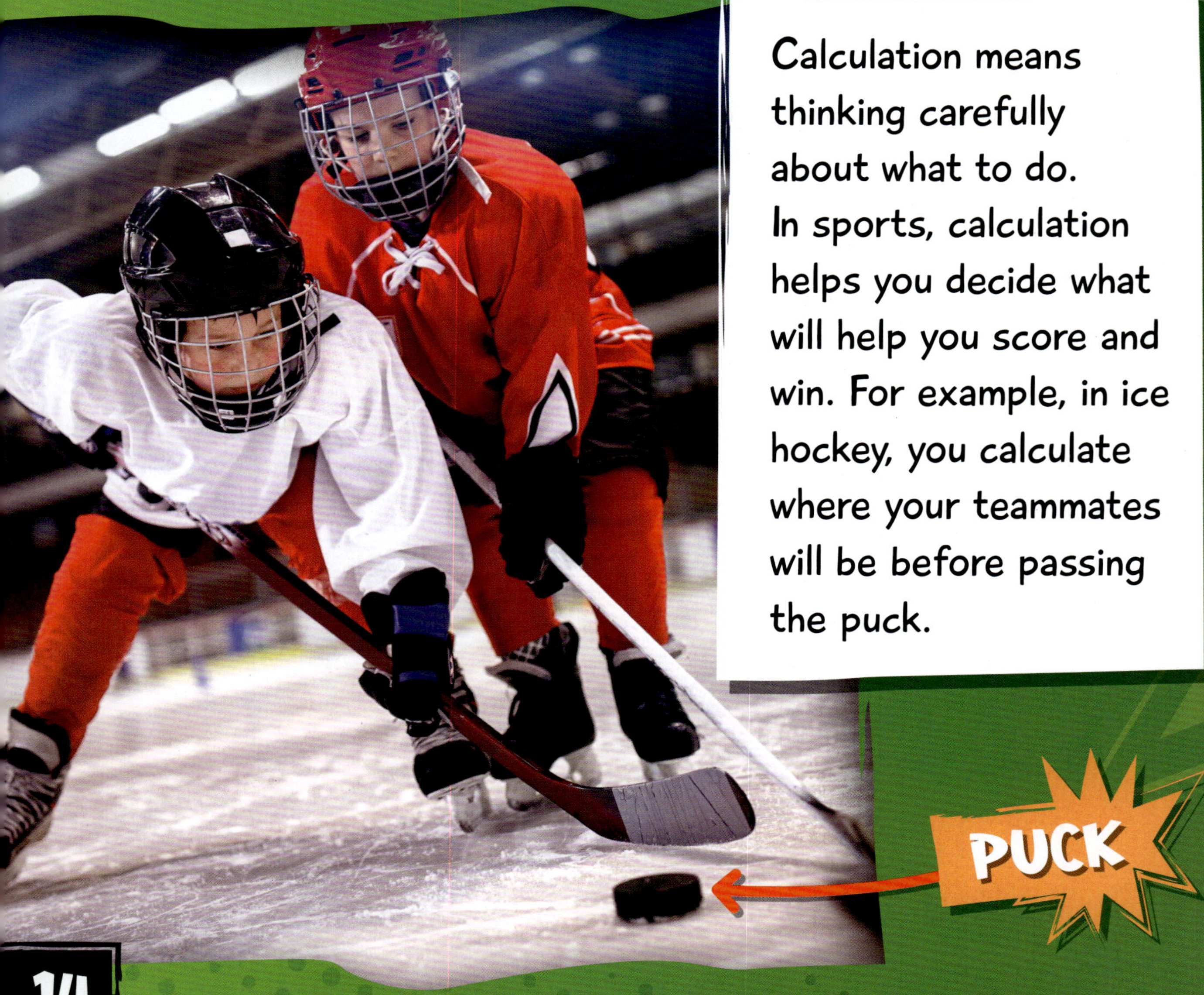

Calculation means thinking carefully about what to do. In sports, calculation helps you decide what will help you score and win. For example, in ice hockey, you calculate where your teammates will be before passing the puck.

In soccer, you think about what speed and direction you need to kick the ball to score a goal. You need to think about where the goalie is too. Using calculated thinking helps you make smarter choices.

PROBLEM SOLVING

Problem solving means figuring out how to fix a problem or overcome a challenge. In auto racing, drivers handle problems such as tricky weather by changing how they turn and how fast they go.

In **equestrian** sports, riders solve problems when their horses do not do what they are told. They figure out if something is bothering the horse and find a solution.

Problem solving is a skill that can help in all parts of life.

SPECIAL EQUIPMENT

Some sports use special equipment. Learning how to use this equipment, and how to do it safely, is a skill. Archery uses bows. It takes skill to hold, use, and take care of these properly.

All kinds of equipment are used in water sports. It takes skill to use paddles and oars to push yourself through water.

Each type of special equipment needs skill to use and handle.

TECHNIQUE

Technique means the way that someone does something. Having good technique is often just as important as being fast or strong. It takes time and effort to learn and improve your technique.

Improving your technique might mean listening to advice from others, such as a coach. Being able to listen to feedback from others and apply it is a skill too.

SUPER SKILLS!

There are all kinds of skills you can learn by getting active. Learning the right skills for your sport helps you play better and have more fun.

Getting active helps your body grow strong and healthy. The more you practice, the more skills you learn and the more fun you will have! So let's get active!

GLOSSARY

COMMUNICATING	passing information between two or more people
EQUESTRIAN	to do with riding horses
FEEDBACK	information about how something could be made better
INNER EARS	the parts of the ear inside the head that control hearing and balance
JOINTS	parts in the body where two or more bones meet
MUSCLES	the parts of the body that help it move

INDEX